KINGFISHER
READERS

level 4

D1124021

Pirates

Philip Steele

KINGFISHER

First published 2012 by Kingfisher
an imprint of Macmillan Children's Books
a division of Macmillan Publishers Limited
20 New Wharf Road, London N1 9RR
Basingstoke and Oxford
Associated companies throughout the world
www.panmacmillan.com

Series editor: Heather Morris
Literacy consultant: Hilary Horton

ISBN: 978-0-7534-3061-3
Copyright © Macmillan Publishers Ltd 2012

9 8 7 6 5 4 3 2

2TR/1011/WKT/UNTD/105MA

A CIP catalogue record for this book is available from
the British Library.

Printed in China

Picture credits
The Publisher would like to thank the following for permission to reproduce their material. Every care has
been taken to trace copyright holders. However, if there have been unintentional omissions or failure to trace
copyright holders, we apologise and will, if informed, endeavour to make corrections in any future edition
(t = top, b = bottom, c = centre, r = right, l = left):
Pages 4–5 Corbis/Joel W. Rogers; 7 Alamy/Lebrecht Music and Arts Photo Library; 25t The Art Archive;
28 Bridgeman Art Library/Peter Newark Historical Pictures; 29 Corbis/Richard T. Nowitz; all other images
from the Kingfisher artbank.

Contents

Pirate attack!

Imagine you are a sailor living about 300 years ago. You have been at sea for many weeks and you haven't seen another ship in all that time. Suddenly a sail appears on the horizon. Does it belong to a friend or an enemy? As the ship gets nearer, you realise it is full of pirates who are getting ready to cut your throat!

Pirates are people who attack ships at sea. They may steal precious rings or jewellery. They may carry off valuable **cargo**, or take the whole ship and sail off in it. Pirates may take people prisoner, or even murder them. There have been pirates as long as people have sailed in boats, and in almost every part of the world. And there are still pirates today.

Pirate speak

Pirates and sailors living 300 years ago had their own special slang. They called the sea bed, with all its sunken shipwrecks, 'Davy Jones's locker'.

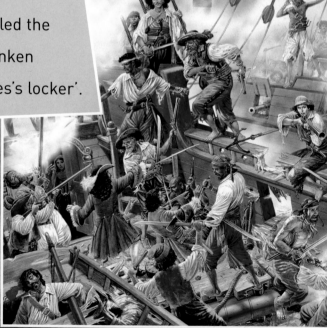

Pirate attacks were terrifying. The pirates fought with pistols and swords.

Who became pirates?

People became pirates for all sorts of reasons. Some, like many **buccaneers**, were violent criminals who had escaped from jail. The buccaneers settled on the Caribbean islands in the 1600s.

Bartholomew Roberts was a Welsh pirate who made lots of money.

Roche Brasiliano

The cruellest buccaneer of all was a Dutchman called Roche Brasiliano. He roasted his Spanish enemies alive!

Some pirates started out as **mutineers**. These were sailors who rebelled against their captain. A Scottish sailor called John Gow led a **mutiny** in 1724. He murdered his ship's officers and became a pirate. Gow was soon feared by sailors from Spain to Scotland.

Some pirates started out as very poor people who just wanted to get rich. Before they sailed, pirate crews agreed how they would share out any treasure they stole. They also agreed to pay crew members who were wounded in the fighting.

Pirates or privateers?

When was a pirate not a pirate?
When he was a **privateer**!
Kings, queens or governments
often gave sea captains, called
privateers, special permission to
attack ships that belonged to
enemies of their country.

In 1523, a French captain called
Jean Fleury captured two Spanish
ships as they sailed home from the
Caribbean. Jean carried off piles of gold,
but he claimed that he was a privateer not
a pirate, and he had letters to prove it.

A big bang!
Welsh rogue Henry Morgan was a buccaneer
and a privateer, too. In 1669 his crew blew up
their own ship by mistake, killing 250 people
on board. They had all drunk too much rum.

Jean Fleury attacks the Spanish treasure ships.

Seafarers were often seen as heroes in their own country but as pirates in another. Between 1577 and 1580, an English sea captain called Francis Drake sailed round the world. On the way he attacked Spanish ships. When he came home he was **knighted** by Queen Elizabeth I of England. The Spanish were furious.

Pirate women

Most sailors thought it was unlucky to have any women on board a ship at sea. Even so, some women did fight on pirate ships, often more fiercely than the men.

Grace O'Malley lived on the west coast of Ireland in the 1560s. She and her crews attacked ships up and down the coast. When the English complained about her piracy, she sailed to London and demanded to meet Queen Elizabeth I face to face! They got on rather well.

Mary Read was
an English pirate
who sailed to the
Caribbean in 1719.
Her ship was captured by another pirate called
John Rackham, or 'Calico Jack'. Mary happily
joined his crew, which included Jack's
girlfriend, Anne Bonny. Mary and Anne
both fought fiercely with
axes and swords.

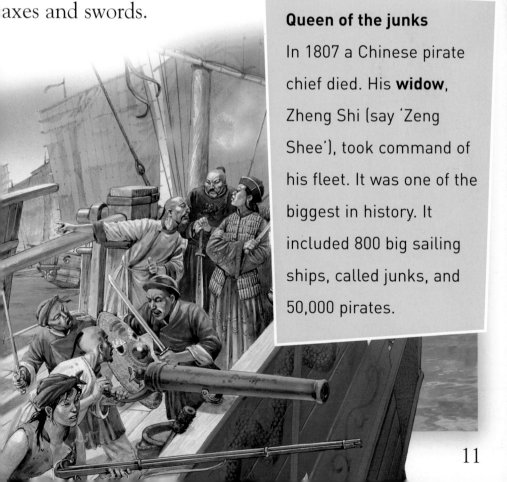

Queen of the junks

In 1807 a Chinese pirate chief died. His **widow**, Zheng Shi (say 'Zeng Shee'), took command of his fleet. It was one of the biggest in history. It included 800 big sailing ships, called junks, and 50,000 pirates.

Pirate ships

Pirate ships have always looked much the same as other ships. After all, they were often ordinary ships that the pirates had stolen and given a new name. Pirates preferred ships that were fast and able to change direction easily in case they had to make a quick getaway. They also needed ships that were small enough to hide away in **inlets** and bays.

Blackbeard

The English pirate called Blackbeard had a ship with 300 pirates and 40 cannon. When he boarded a ship he was a terrifying sight because he wore smoking fuses in his hair.

The **Barbary corsairs** were pirates from North Africa, in the 1500s. They used fast boats called **galleys**, which had sails and oars. The prisoners they captured were chained, and forced to row as galley **slaves**.

In the 1600s the buccaneers often used long, low sailing canoes. In the 1700s pirates in North America and the Caribbean preferred speedy sailing ships called **sloops** or **schooners**.

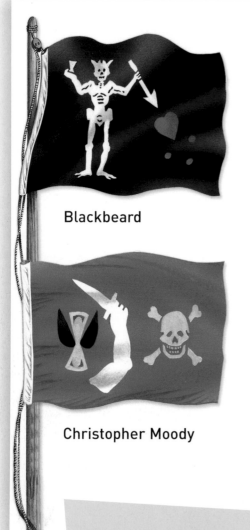

Blackbeard

Christopher Moody

Flags of death

The Barbary corsairs flew red flags on their galleys. Other pirates also chose red, the colour of blood, for their ships. The flags meant one thing: expect no mercy! Later, pirate flags were often coloured black and red, black and white, or plain black. They were known as **blackjacks** or **Jolly Rogers**.

Tricks and trickery

Sometimes pirates used tricks to take over a ship. They raised the flag of a country to fool their victims as they approached them. Then at the last moment they would raise the pirate flag instead.

John Rackham, or Calico Jack

Henry Avery

Many pirate captains flew their own personal flags. Calico Jack's flag design was a skull with crossed **cutlasses**. An English pirate captain called Henry Avery flew a flag with a skull and crossbones design. The flag of Bartholomew Roberts showed himself holding hands with a skeleton. It must have scared a lot of people because this Welsh pirate captured over 470 ships!

Bartholomew Roberts

Thomas Tew

Life at sea

Pirates had to be good sailors. They had to **navigate**, using the sun or stars to find their way, and read charts. They had to climb the mast in the middle of a storm to raise or lower sails. They needed to be able to handle all sorts of weapons, such as pistols, swords, knives and axes.

Sometimes pirates had to haul their ship up onto a beach, to clean the hull or repair broken timbers. This was a dangerous time because if they were spotted by a **navy patrol**, they could not get away.

Sometimes there were drunken quarrels and fights. In 1697, Captain William Kidd had a blazing row with his gunner, William Moore. Kidd killed him with a single blow to the head using a bucket.

Disgusting dishes!
During a long voyage, the food could be revolting. The biscuits were hard and full of creepy-crawlies. Meat was made very salty to stop it going rotten.

The crew repair leaks and mend a broken rudder.

Chests of treasure

Pirates preferred treasure that was easy to transport, easy to divide among themselves, and easy to sell. The best treasure was gold or silver coins, bars of metal, jewellery or weapons.

Gold and silver coins in the Caribbean were called **pieces of eight, doubloons** and **moidores**. A French pirate called Antonio Fuët once ran out of cannonballs, so he loaded his guns with gold coins instead. After that, they called him Captain Moidore.

Some pirate captains stole fancy pieces of clothing to wear so they could show off. They liked wearing gold **braid**, lace cuffs, or **plumed** hats.

One of the biggest treasure hauls ever was by the English pirate Henry or Long Ben Avery. In 1695 he attacked Indian ships in the Red Sea. They belonged to the Indian emperor and were loaded with treasure. The attack was very brutal and violent, and Long Ben made a fortune.

Pirate tales often tell of treasure chests buried on lonely islands, or of secret pirate maps. These are mostly just stories, but people keep searching without any luck!

These pirates are burying treasure on an island.

Pirate havens

Pirates need safe places, called havens, to anchor and unload their boats. These havens are usually in remote areas, where the pirates can live and sell their **spoils** without being caught. There used to be pirate havens in many parts of the world.

One pirate base was Port Royal in Jamaica. From 1655, buccaneers anchored there. It became a drunken, lawless place.

Port Royal, Jamaica, in the 1660s.

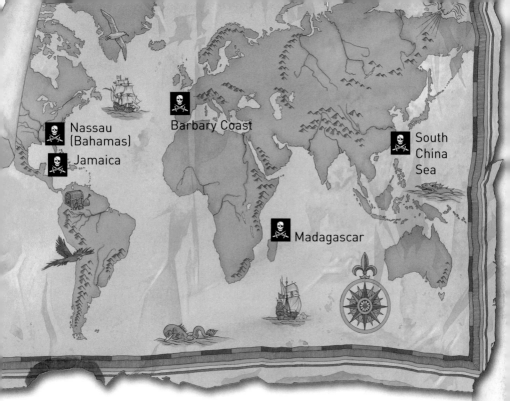

The map shows the locations labeled:
- Nassau (Bahamas)
- Jamaica
- Barbary Coast
- South China Sea
- Madagascar

The island of Madagascar, off the coast of Africa, was also popular with pirates. One of them was named Abraham Samuel. He was on a voyage from the Indian Ocean to New York when he was shipwrecked in Madagascar. He ruled here as a king, from 1697 to 1705.

This map shows popular havens for pirates in the 1600s and 1700s.

Ruled by pirates

Between 1614 and 1660 the port of Salé in Morocco, North Africa, was ruled by Barbary corsairs. These pirates went raiding as far away as England, Iceland and Newfoundland.

Terrible deeds

Today we read all sorts of exciting stories about pirates. We sometimes forget that, really, piracy was horrible and brutal, and that it still is today.

Chinese pirates sometimes nailed their victims to the deck. The pirates of Borneo often chopped off their victims' heads. In the 1600s a buccaneer, called François l'Ollonois, used his cutlass to cut out his enemy's heart.

The pirate who was too kind

The pirate Edward England was different from most pirates because he often spared his victims' lives. When Edward refused to kill the crew of an English ship, his own crew **marooned** him on an island as a punishment.

The Barbary corsairs often held their victims as prisoners and would not let them go until someone paid a fee called a **ransom**.

Sometimes pirates left their victims on desert islands, where they might starve to death. This was called marooning. Often pirates just set their prisoners **adrift** at sea in a small boat, with very little food.

These pirates are demanding a ransom from a wealthy man they have captured.

Pirate hunters

As long as pirates have existed, they have been hunted down, captured and killed. Navies sent out patrols to seek out the worst pirates.

In 1718, the British navy caught Blackbeard in North Carolina. He was very strong and received 25 wounds by pistol and cutlass before falling down. His head was chopped off and hung from the front of the ship.

Bartholomew Roberts was found on the African coast by *HMS Swallow*, in 1722. There was a fight and he was shot in the throat. At the time he was wearing a crimson waistcoat and his fanciest clothes. His crew buried him at sea before the navy could take away his body.

British ships attack the junks of the Chinese pirates.

Sometimes there were big battles with whole fleets of pirate ships. In 1849, the British navy fought a great battle against Chinese pirates near Hong Kong. About 400 pirates were killed.

The pirates' biggest defeat

In 66BCE, the Romans went to war with pirates in the Mediterranean Sea. They captured 20,000 of them and killed 10,000 more.

Punishment and death

A few pirates won fame and fortune, but most died in battle, drowned, or ended up as beggars.

Many pirates were brought to trial in a court of law. If they were found guilty, they were normally severely punished. Some pirates had their head cut off. Some were shot. Most often, pirates were hanged in public. Their dead bodies were left hanging in iron cages by the port, as a warning to all who sailed by.

Dragged to death

William de Marisco attacked ships in the Irish Sea. He was captured on Lundy island in 1242. He was dragged through the streets of London by horses. His body was chopped into four pieces and burned.

A pirate's body hangs in an iron cage so no one can take it and bury him properly.

27

Glossary

adrift Floating on the sea.

Barbary corsairs Pirates from the North African coast, who sailed from the 1500s to the 1800s.

blackjack A pirate flag of the 1690s and 1700s, such as the skull-and-crossbones.

braid Decorative strands or plaits of thread, often in silver or gold.

buccaneers Caribbean pirates of the 1600s.

cargo The goods carried by ships.

cutlass A deadly slashing sword used by sailors from the 1600s onwards.

doubloon An old Spanish gold coin.

galleys Wooden ships that use oars as well as sails.

inlet Part of the coast that forms a narrow bay.

Jolly Roger Any pirate flag, especially the skull-and-crossbones.

knighted Given the title 'Sir'.

maroon To leave someone behind on an island.

moidore An old gold coin used in Portugal and Brazil.

mutineer A sailor or soldier who disobeys orders.

mutiny A rebellion against ships' officers or army officers.

navigate To find one's way, or keep a ship on course.

navy A country's warships and their crews.

patrol A group of sailors or soldiers sent to look out for enemies.

pieces of eight Old Spanish coins.

plumed Having a fancy feather or crest.

privateer A captain who is given special permission to attack certain ships.

ransom A sum of money paid to set a prisoner free.

rogue A wicked person.

schooner A small, fast sailing ship, usually with two masts.

seafarer A sailor or mariner, someone who goes to sea.

slave Someone whose freedom is taken away, and who is forced to work for no money.

sloop A small, fast sailing ship with one mast.

spoils Money made from crime, or stolen treasure.

widow A woman whose husband has died.

Index